3 1994 01313 4868

SANT

D0742854

AR PTS: 0.5

BLAZERS

MILITARY VEHICLES

U.S.
AIR FORCE
BOMBERS

by Carrie A. Braulick

Reading Consultant:
Barbara J. Fox
Reading Specialist
North Carolina State University

J 623.7463 BRA
Braulick, Carrie A.
U.S. Air Force bombers

$19.93
CENTRAL   31994013134868

Blazers is published by Capstone Press,
151 Good Counsel Drive, P.O. Box 669, Mankato, Minnesota 56002.
www.capstonepress.com

Copyright © 2006 by Capstone Press. All rights reserved.
No part of this publication may be reproduced in whole or in part, or stored in a retrieval system, or transmitted in any form or by any means, electronic, mechanical, photocopying, recording, or otherwise, without written permission of the publisher. For information regarding permission, write to Capstone Press, 151 Good Counsel Drive, P.O. Box 669, Dept. R, Mankato, Minnesota 56002. Printed in the United States of America

Library of Congress Cataloging-in-Publication Data
Braulick, Carrie A., 1975–
    U.S. Air Force bombers/by Carrie A. Braulick.
    p. cm.—(Blazers. Military vehicles)
    Summary: "Provides an overview of the design, uses, weapons, and equipment of U.S. Air Force bombers"—Provided by publisher.
    Includes bibliographical references and index.
    ISBN-13: 978-0-7368-5466-5 (hardcover)
    ISBN-10: 0-7368-5466-5 (hardcover)
    1. Bombers—United States—Juvenile literature. 2. United States. Air Force—Equipment and supplies—Juvenile literature. I. Title. II. Series.
UG1242.B6B69 2006
623.74'63'0973—dc22   2005016441

Editorial Credits
Jenny Marks, editor; Thomas Emery, designer; Jo Miller,
    photo researcher/photo editor

Photo Credits
Corbis, 20; Aero Graphics Inc., 14, 25, 27; George Hall, 11 (both)
DVIC/SSGT Jerry Morrison, 28–29; TSGT Michael R. Nixon, 17
Getty Images Inc./Julian Herbert, 9
Photo by Ted Carlson/Fotodynamics, 5, 7 (bottom), 12–13, 22–23
Photo by U.S. Air Force, (cover), 7 (top), 19 (both), 21, 26; Tech Sgt.
    Cecilio Ricardo, 15

Special thanks to Raymond L. Puffer, PhD, Historian, Air Force Flight Test Center, Edwards Air Force Base, California, for his assistance in preparing this book.

1 2 3 4 5 6 11 10 09 08 07 06

TABLE OF CONTENTS

Air Force
Bombers

A U.S. Air Force bomber sweeps low over enemy land. Enemies do not know the bomber is above them until it is too late.

Air Force bombers are a threat to enemies everywhere. They fly thousands of miles to send bombs smashing into targets.

BLAZER FACT

A B-52 bomber completed the longest combat mission ever flown by a U.S. military plane. It flew for 35 hours.

DESIGN

Bombers are huge and heavy. At least four powerful engines help them build speed. Other planes have only one or two engines.

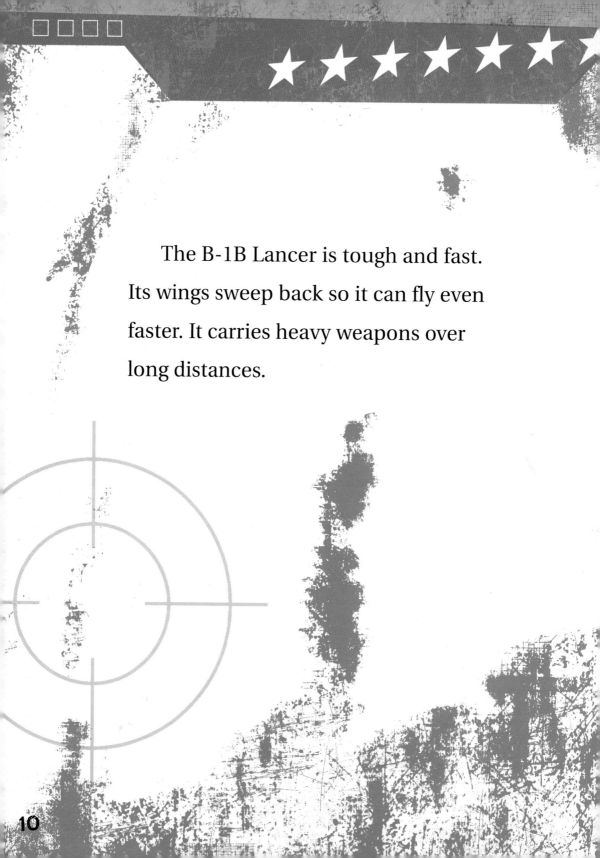

The B-1B Lancer is tough and fast. Its wings sweep back so it can fly even faster. It carries heavy weapons over long distances.

BLAZER FACT

Pilots call the B-52 the "Big Ugly Fat Fellow."

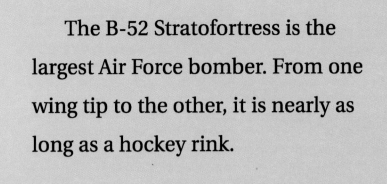

The B-52 Stratofortress is the largest Air Force bomber. From one wing tip to the other, it is nearly as long as a hockey rink.

The B-2 Spirit looks like a giant
wing. The sharp angles of the B-2
keep it hidden from enemy radar.

WEAPONS AND EQUIPMENT

Bombers use different weapons to blast away targets. Crew members load the weapons into the bomb bay.

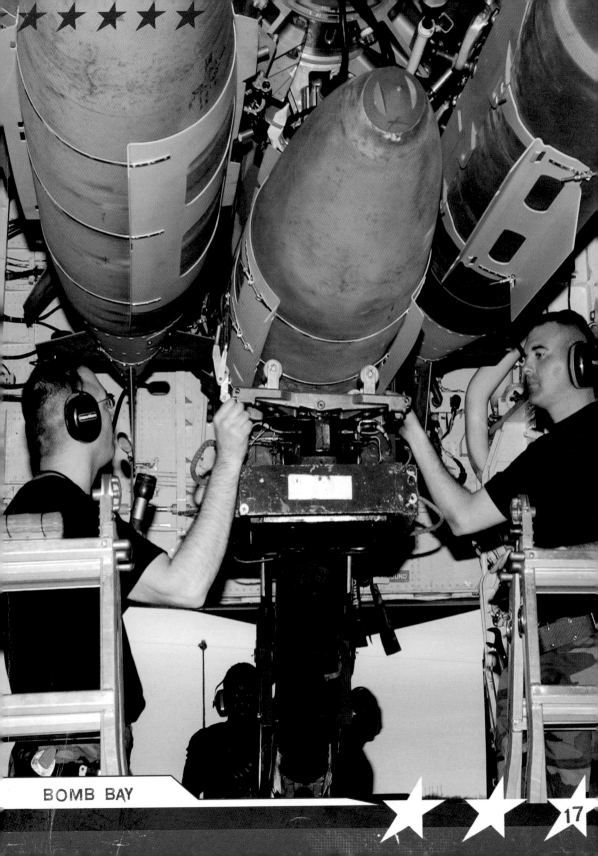

BOMB BAY

Cluster bombs destroy large **areas.**
Pilots drop several cluster bombs
at once. Those bombs release many
smaller bombs as they fall.

BLAZER FACT

Bombers use Joint Direct
Attack Munitions (JDAMs) to
bomb small targets. JDAMs
are deadly and accurate.

CLUSTER BOMBS

JDAM

B-1B COCKP

Pilots use cockpit controls to fly bombers. Computers help pilots avoid mountains or trees in their path.

BLAZER FACT

A computer keeps the B-2 steady. The wing flaps are adjusted up to 40 times each second.

B-1B BOMBER

WING

REAR OF ENGINES

TAIL

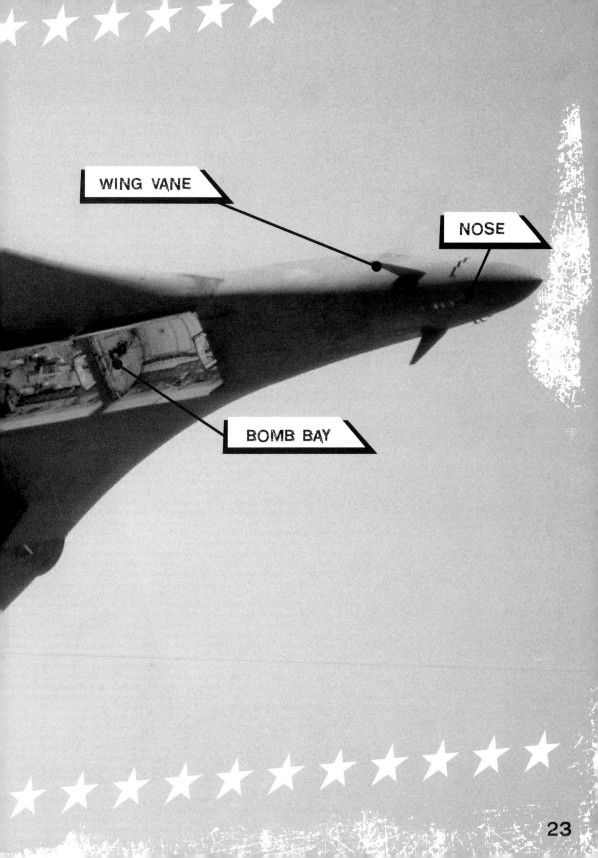

WING VANE

NOSE

BOMB BAY

BOMBERS IN FLIGHT

A pilot and copilot fly bombers. The B-52 has extra crew members to fire weapons and watch for enemy attacks.

Tanker planes refuel bombers on long missions. Bombers travel day and night to reach their targets. Nothing can stop these amazing airplanes!

★ ★ ★ ★ ★

IN-FLIGHT REFUELING

BLAZER FACT

B-2 pilots and copilots take turns taking short naps during long flights.

HIGH-SOARING B-1BS!

GLOSSARY

bomb bay (BOM BAY)—the storage area in a bomber where the bombs are held

cockpit (KOK-pit)—the area in front of a plane where the pilot sits

mission (MISH-uhn)—a military task

radar (RAY-dar)—equipment that uses radio waves to locate and guide objects

tanker plane (TANG-kur PLAYNE)—a plane that carries extra fuel tanks for refueling other planes

target (TAR-git)—something that is aimed for or shot at

READ MORE

Berliner, Don. *Stealth Fighters and Bombers.*
Aircraft. Berkeley Heights, N.J.: Enslow, 2001.

Dartford, Mark. *Bombers.* Military Hardware in
Action. Minneapolis: Lerner, 2003.

Green, Michael, and Gladys Green. *Heavy
Bombers: The B-52 Stratofortresses.* War Planes.
Mankato, Minn.: Capstone Press, 2004.

INTERNET SITES

FactHound offers a safe, fun way
to find Internet sites related
to this book. All of the sites
on FactHound have been
researched by our staff.

Here's how:

1. Visit www.facthound.com
2. Type in this special code **0736854665**
   for age-appropriate sites. Or enter a search
   word related to this book for a more general
   search.
3. Click on the **Fetch It** button.

FactHound will fetch the best sites for you!

INDEX